The Passionate Entrepreneur's Strategies

An Entrepreneurship Guide that Reveals How to Grow Multiple Income Streams, Create Good Customer Relationship with Business Quotes & Advice for Beginners

**Lucrative Business Ideas Series
Book 1**

Buzzer Joseph

Copyright © 2020

Buzzer Joseph

All Rights Reserved

No part of this book may be reproduced in any form without a written permission from the author. Reviewers are allowed to quote brief passages of the content of this book in their review write-ups.

Legal Disclaimer

The information contained in this book are business advice that for motivating young entrepreneurs. Most of them worked for the author. But there is no guarantee that it will yield the same result for you.

The author and publisher disclaim any liability arising directly or indirectly from the use of this book.

DEDICATION

This book is dedicated to God for giving me the inspiration to write this book for all young entrepreneurs who wish to know the right way to start their entrepreneurship lifestyle.

Table of Contents

INTRODUCTION 7

THE JOYS OF LIVING AN ENTREPRENEUR LIFESTYLE: MY ENTREPRENEURSHIP STARTUP STORY 10

ENTREPRENEUR VS. EMPLOYEE 15

An Entrepreneur 15

An Employee 15

Savings vs. Investments 16

WHY 99% OF YOUNG ENTREPRENEURS FAIL IN BUSINESS 18

HOW TO JOIN THE 1% SUCCESSFUL ENTREPRENEURS 24

ENTREPRENEURSHIP SKILLS VS. JOB SKILLS 45

Best Ways to Improve your Skills as an Entrepreneur 45

The Best Time to Quit your Job 46

HOW TO DISCOVER THE BUSINESS IDEAS THAT WILL WORK FOR YOU 49

HOW TO USE SWOT ANALYSIS FOR EFFECTIVE BUSINESS PLANNING 54

Elements of SWOT Analysis 54

How to Create a Prioritized SWOT List 57

How to Use the Results of SWOT Analysis for Effective Business Planning 59

Why Every Business Needs SWOT Analysis 60

HOW TO OVERCOME THE MAIN BUSINESS STARTUP CHALLENGES: CAPITAL AND RUNNING FUNDS 62

Best Ways to Raise Fund for Business Startup 62

Tips for Saving Money at the Early Stage of your Business 67

HOW TO BUILD A GOOD RELATIONSHIP WITH YOUR CUSTOMERS AND EMPLOYEES 69

Why should you Value your Customers? 69

Simple Rules for Retaining Customers 71

Best Ways to Appreciate your Employees 71

HOW TO CREATE SUCCESSFUL MULTIPLE PASSIVE INCOME STREAMS 76

Various Forms of Wealth and Assets 78

Business Ideas for Entrepreneurs 79

The 8 Income Streams for Entrepreneurs 90

INSPIRING BUSINESS QUOTES AND ADVICE FOR YOUNG ENTREPRENEURS 92

A QUIZ FOR YOU 100

CONCLUSION 101

YOUR NEXT READ: ENTREPRENEURS MULTIPLE INCOME STREAMS GUIDES 102

BONUS: FREE ENTREPRENEURSHIP RESOURCES FOR FURTHER INSIGHT 103

Entrepreneurship Startup Guide & Business Advice 103

Skill Acquisition & Business Ideas 107

INTRODUCTION

The life of an entrepreneur has never been a bed of roses and will never be - A hard truth which you will not hear from many successful entrepreneur! Only those who know the challenges they will meet on the entrepreneurship journey and are determined to face these challenges, without having *the give up* mindset as an option succeed. You also need self-discipline because it will help you avoid distractions and focus on your goals.

But how can you know the type of challenges to expect in the journey? The easiest way is to learn from those who have passed through the process. I started my entrepreneurship journey right back in 2014 and today, am happy with the success I have made so far as an author, blogger and digital marketer. Am also happy for the number of times I failed because they taught me lessons that made me a successful entrepreneur. Although no two entrepreneurs can have the same life and business challenges, but they may have similar challenges. How can you learn from failure if you don't expect and plan for it right from the onset?

This book ***The Passionate Entrepreneur's Strategies*** will answer the following questions and more:

- What signs will I see and know that a business idea will succeed or fail?
- How can I discover a business idea that will be successful?
- Why do 99% of young entrepreneurs fail?
- How can I be among the 1% successful young entrepreneurs?
- What business advice do successful entrepreneurs have for a beginner like me?
- Which skills will give me the greater chance to succeed as an entrepreneur?
- How can I make effective business planning with SWOT analysis?
- What are the best ways to overcome these main startup business challenges: capital and running funds?
- How can I successfully create and manage multiple businesses?
- How can I attract new customers and retain existing customers in my business?

You will also discover books and movies for entrepreneurs, especially beginners. Unlike most entrepreneurship and business books, I gave you as a bonus, some free resources to help you start putting to practice all that you have learnt in this book because I believe that **only actions can yield the desired results, not just reading.**

Now explore this book and start successful businesses that will yield multiple income streams.

Best regards,

Buzzer Joseph

THE JOYS OF LIVING AN ENTREPRENEUR LIFESTYLE: MY ENTREPRENEURSHIP STARTUP STORY

I have tried many times to see if I could adopt the employees' lifestyle. But I certainly couldn't. Imagine waking up everyday by 3 pm, leaving my house by 5:30 am and getting to the office by 7:30 am just to avoid being fired. I also try to imagine over-working myself and getting a penny, while another man who just sits in an office, coming to work whenever he wishes takes the glory.

I made this decision to become an entrepreneur even before I stepped into the four walls of the campus. A night before packing to the campus, I woke up around 4 pm, thinking about what life holds for me as an undergraduate. Then this big question came into my mind, "***If you are given an opportunity to either be the best graduating student in your set without any skill or being a full entrepreneur without making first class, which one will you go for***"?

I thought about this for almost 30 minutes. I recalled my Dad's advice a night before, "Please my son, make me proud in the university". So I asked myself, "Which option will make him more proud? Graduating with the best grade with no skill or being an established young man even before I graduate"?

I also recalled the advice Jack Ma gave his son, "***You don't need to be among the top three in your class, being in the middle is fine, so long as your grades are not too bad. Only this kind of person has enough free time to learn new skills***".

My Dad was successful as an employee, but I wanted to be an Entrepreneur. So I decided to follow the advice of a successful entrepreneur. That same night, I made a great decision which helped me actualize my dream. I made my Dad proud, not as an employee, but as an entrepreneur.

I graduated with a good grade, though not a first class grade. A second class upper grade, with blogging, book writing and digital marketing skills. In fact, I made my first 7 figure income as an undergraduate. Is that not pretty cool? The truth remains that all these achievements never came on a platter of gold. I paid a price.

The joy of waking up whenever I wish, planning and using my time as I wish, not being over worried with how I would satisfy someone else just to make a living is the most valuable thing that I have got in this world.

Before I got admission into university, I worked as an Assistant Computer Engineer in one renowned computer center in my area. Due to lack of workers, I was given extra duties; attending to all customers in the cyber café section, going to buy petrol for the generator, taking passport photograph, which I willingly accepted and carried out diligently.

After 2 months with the company, the manager called me a day before our payment-receiving date. He said, "Joseph, we are facing some financial challenges in this company and to make sure we don't go out of business, we have decided to pay workers according to their output. After analyzing your duties in this company, we have decided to reduce your salary be half. Am sorry, because the decision has been finalized and nothing could be done about it".

That was the worst day of my life. But am happy because that was the day I stopped thinking as an employee and made the decision to be my own boss. I left the company at the end of the same month. That was the last company I worked as a full-time worker. I started making plans on how to start this great lifestyle, how to overcome the challenges I might face. Those plans helped me discover the great potentials in me.

I know you might have had a similar life story. But what decision did you make; to study hard, make the best result, get a good job? No, you could achieve something better if you take the other route – **the entrepreneurship route.**

The average annual salaries of the middle class citizens of the United States is around $50,000. To reach the top 25% of income earners, you need to earn at least $100,000 a year. To reach the top 10%, you must earn at least $150,000 a year. To join the top 5% class, you must earn at least $200,000 a year. If you wish to join the top 1%, you must earn a combined household income of at least $400,000 a year.

So now answer this question: **What do you think will give you the best chance the move up and join the top 10%, 5% and 1%?** Is it a salary increase? Not at all. You could easily achieve this by being your own boss - an entrepreneur.

Entrepreneurs avoid the rat race because they know that anyone who wins the rat race is still a rat. **Are you a rat?**

ENTREPRENEUR VS. EMPLOYEE

You need to have a clear view about an entrepreneur and employee, what distinguishes them, their lifestyles and reaction towards challenges.

An Entrepreneur

An entrepreneur is an individual who refused to entrust their future into the hands of a fellow individual. He sees problems as challenges which have solutions and once solved, will take him to the next higher level. He is well educated even if he did not have the privilege to go to school. He believes that life is the greatest teacher who never stops teaching people lessons. He creates his own economy and decides how it will be at any point in time.

An Employee

An employee on the other hand is an individual who prefers to depend on his fellow individual because he is afraid of the future. He prefers to be paid monthly salaries and will displease himself in order to please his employee. He might go to school and get the best and highest degree but he is not educated. He believes that the greatest teacher is their school professor. His future depends on the economy of his country.

Savings vs. Investments

Savings and investment are what differentiate a true entrepreneur from an employee. But most entrepreneurs still ask, "Between saving and investment, which one should I give a higher priority"? I have decided not to answer this question directly because I believe you could find a better understanding if you understand the features of each term.

Here are what you should know about savings and investments:

For Savings:

- It is short term.
- The risk is very minimal, but the returns is very small.
- It cannot keep up with inflation.
- The returns are the interests you earn from banks
- You don't need any skill to save.

For Investment:

- It is long term.
- The risk is very high, likewise the returns.
- It can comfortably keep up with inflation.
- It returns dividends and profits.
- You need a skill in order to invest wisely.

I hope that by now, you have known the one to give the higher priority? In business, money kept in the bank is called a "dead money" because it is not adding any value to your own economy as an entrepreneur. You can only teach money how to work for you by investing it.

Investment might seem riskier than saving, but also know that the higher the risk, the higher the returns. But make sure you fully understand the system where you are planning to invest your money. You could keep back the money in the bank until you have properly understood the key aspects of the business you wish to invest in. Understand the risks and the gains.

WHY 99% OF YOUNG ENTREPRENEURS FAIL IN BUSINESS

Do you wish to know why almost all who wish to become entrepreneurs fail? Here are some of the top reasons:

Ineffective Planning

There are two main types of business planning: long-term and short-term planning. If you neglect long-term planning, your business might show signs of success at the beginning, but will surely fail at the long run. Always include goals and results. They will help you know if your business is actually making progress or not.

Bad Leadership

No business will ever survive with bad leadership. If you have poor leadership skills as an entrepreneur, you will always make poor decisions in every aspect of your business. How do you improve your leadership skills as an entrepreneur? By learning. You learn most times through reading and asking questions. How can you learn when you don't ask question?

Lack of Good Business Mentors

You cannot improve your leadership skills by seeking for help from any source. What does a fruit seller has to offer in investment and business decision-making? Very little, if there anything at all. Connect with successful entrepreneurs in your business field. Ask them how they were able to solve similar challenges you are facing.

Trying to Imitate your Competitors with any Differentiation

It is recommended to know your competitors and know what they do. But it is never advisable to imitate them without any differentiation. The reason for knowing what your competitors do is to help you improve your brand. Differentiation is what makes a business products unique from those of their competitors. If you already have a great product, then develop a unique proposition, else you will get lost in the competition.

Poor Customer Support

More than 80% of businesses that failed was due to poor customer support. Customers are always looking for where they will get maximum satisfaction. If they don't get help from your business when they need it, they are bound to leave your company. As I mentioned earlier, it is not all about acquiring new customers, but your ability to retain your existing customers. If you want to build a successful business empire, then you must have a hyper-active customer support section.

Inability to Learn from previous Failures

Prepare to fail. Failure is part of every business. The lessons you gained from your failed business idea are what will help you build a successful business. Successful entrepreneurs see failure as challenges and this helped them readjust their mindset when looking for solutions.

Wrong Start-up and Expansion Strategies

There is a procedure for everything, likewise in business. If you must succeed, you need a startup strategy. One of the key features of a good start-up is knowing the right start-up scale. Most business fail because they started in large scale, then on the long run, they were unable to cope with the challenges of a large scale business and they fail. It is always advisable to start in a small scale and then grow gradually. If you try to grow very fast, even with a good start-up scale, your business will still fail. That was happened to **Pet.com**. They tried to go worldwide too soon. Guess what? They also crashed too soon.

Poor Management Skills

The two most important aspect of business management are **inventory** and **financial** management. Too little and too much inventory will hurt your business profitability.

The same applies to financial management. You need to keep adequate records of all your business finances so that you will be able to make effective decisions. Always go for professional accounting software like QuickBooks, FreshBooks, etc. If you don't have a ground knowledge in business finance, hire a professional.

Lack of Adequate Capital and Business Running Funds

Inadequate startup funds has led many young businesses to their early grave. Some other businesses fail because their owner borrowed a long-term loan to startup the business which takes more time to break even. When the loan repayment time comes and the loan is paid back, the business runs out of funds. The management could not even afford the day-to-day running cost. Within a short period, the business folds.

As an entrepreneur, always go for long-term loan if your business plan predicts that the business will take a longer time to break even. Loans should be repaid from the company's profit, not from the running capital.

Macroeconomic Factors

There are some factors that are beyond the control of the business owner. Macroeconomic factors are included. These factors include: recessions, wars, natural disasters, inflation, business cycles, etc. Only few companies survive the effect of these factors. The secret is long-term business planning.

Working with the Wrong Team

Inasmuch as a good team work produces more positive result, starting a business with the wrong team will surely kill the business. This is because every business needs the best, especially at its early stage.

Even if it is a partnership business, a wrong business partner will also hurt the business and eventually kill it.

Being Quick to Offer Credit Sales to Customers

If you want to kill the most financially buoyant business, sell on credit. You must be very selective in offering credit to customers. If possible, avoid it at the startup stage of your business. Also have a credit limit for each week. Once reached, don't sell on credit till the next week. Also make sure the debtors are creditworthy.

HOW TO JOIN THE 1% SUCCESSFUL ENTREPRENEURS

Is it still possible to switch from an employee lifestyle to an entrepreneurship lifestyle? Yes, it very much possible. But you need to promise yourself that no matter what happens on the road, you will no change your mind. The process is a full transformation which takes time, may be more than a year. Is it a long time? It is not. In fact, it is nothing compared to working your entire lifetime just to make a living.

The hard truth about entrepreneurship is that it is not meant for everyone. Only 1% out of the 100% that want to be entrepreneurs succeed. Why do these 1% succeed? Simply because they don't give up. When they fail, they try again and again. Also they try to know why they failed. They seek solution from successful entrepreneurs. Then they try a different approach. They read books. They keep trying until they become successful.

Do you wish to be among this one percent that succeed? Are you still living an employee lifestyle but wish to switch over to entrepreneurship? Now do these:

Plan your Time

Both the poor and the rich have the same 24 hours everyday. The only difference is how it is being used. Spend more time learning than having fun. In fact, make learning a fun.

Always plan every minute of your time and follow your plans. There should be time for work out, gist, watching movies, praying and working on your project. But make sure you allocate time to each of these things properly.

Invest more than you Spend

Entrepreneurs spend whatever remains after investing. Employees invest whatever remains after spending. Where do you belong? Do not buy a bag of $650 and have nothing in it. Rather buy a bag of $50 and have $600 in it. Do not pile your money in a bank, let your money work for you. Invest in real estate business, invest in stock market. Invest in things that will have a higher value in the next 5 years.

Do not put your eggs in one basket. Don't invest all your funds in a system such that you will fall back to level zero if the system crashes.

When you hear of a new business opportunity, research and understand how the business works before you invest in it. Understand the escape routes of the business before you invest.

Start with something you love Doing

Passion is what keeps you going until your business succeeds and start paying you. Passion is what motivates you to keep trying. Do you like writing? Then start with book publishing or blogging. Do you love trading, then open your own store.

It is easier to get new ideas on what you love doing than on what you never understood how it works.

You start failing when you start chasing the money instead of a game where you love the process. If you want to become an entrepreneur only because of the money, you should better stick to a job because you will cause more damage than value.

Access your Achievements

One of the ways to know if you are actually making progress is to compare what you have achieved so far with the goals you set earlier. It will help know whether to put more effort on your own or seek for help from others. Ask yourself, "What do I need to make more progress"? If you already have the, then continue working and improving. But the requirements are not within your reach, seek for ways to get them.

Have a Business Mentor

In every business, there are always some individuals who are more successful than the rest. They became more successful because they made more mistakes than other but learnt great lessons from their mistakes. They did not quit.

You need to locate these successful entrepreneurs in your field and get closer to them. Seek opinions and advice from them. Out of ten questions you ask them, they will answer about seven with real life illustrations, most of their personal experience in the system. This is one of the best ways to learn.

How do you get closer to these successful entrepreneurs? The truth is that these gurus are very busy, very time conscious. They are always seeking for new ideas. Come to them with new ideas and ask for better ways to improve the idea. Prove that you already have one. They will share their ideas with you. The more you share ideas, the more you learn smarter ways to improve yourself.

Don't keep looking for the best entrepreneur as a mentor. You need the right mentor, not the best mentor. Look for someone who understands you, and is open-minded, someone who values you, sees a potential in you and is ever ready to help out.

Read Wide

Show me a successful entrepreneur who do not read and I will prove to you that he is an employee, not an entrepreneur. Read books on investment, finance, self-improvement and new business ideas. Warren Buffett gained investment ideas that made him a billionaire by reading financial education books. Never stop learning because life never stops teaching. The day you stop reading is the day you die.

Don't stop reading because you have left school. In fact from the day you left school, you stopped studying and started learning. But you should never stop reading because it one of the surest ways of learning. Each relevant book you read gives you a key to the solution of a new challenge.

Don't just read books without following it up with a positive action. Try to implement some of the ideas you learnt from each book. That is how you can become the better version of yourself.

Here are some I personally recommend for entrepreneurs and business owners:

- *Rich Dad Poor Dad* by Robert T. Kiyosaki
- *Think and Grow Rich* by Napoleon Hill
- *The 7 Habits of Highly Effective People* by Stephen R. Covey
- *The 4-Hour Workweek* by Tim Ferriss
- *The Hard Thing about Hard Things* by Ben Horowitz
- *Start with Why* by Simon Sinek
- *Good to Great* by James C. Collins
- *The Innovator's Dilemma* by Clayton Christensen
- *12 Rules for Life* by Jordan Peterson
- *The Subtle Act of Not Giving a F*ck* by Mark Manson
- *What they won't Teach You* by Andre Haykal Jr
- *The $100 Startup* by Chris Guillebeau
- *The Lean StartUp* by Eric Ries
- *Purple Cow* by Seth Godin
- *Crushing it!* by Gary Vaynerchuk

- *The Four Steps to the Epiphany* by Steve Blank
- *Founders at Work* by Jessica Livingston
- *Built to Last* by Jim Collins & Jerry I. Porras
- *Delivering Happiness* by Tony Hsieh
- *The Power of Broke* by Daymond John
- *The Art of the Start* by Guy Kawasaki
- *Losing my Virginity* by Richard Branson
- *Outliers* by Malcolm Gladwell
- *Deep Work* by Cal Newport
- *The Founder's Dilemma* by Noam T. Wasserman
- *The Millionaire Fastlane* by M.J. DeMarco
- *Tools of Titans* by Tim Ferriss
- *The War Art* by Steven Pressfield
- *The Entrepreneur Mind* by Kevin D. Johnson
- *The Personal MBA* by Josh Kaufman
- *Steve Jobs* by Walter Isaacson
- *Business Adventures* by John Brook
- *The Tipping Point* by Malcolm Gladwell
- *Originals* by Adam Grant
- *The Obstacle is the Way* by Ryan Holiday
- *Shoe Dog* by Phil Knight
- *Grit* by Angela Duckworth
- *Steal like an Artist* by Austin Kleon
- *The Startup Playbook* by David S. Kidder

- *Running Lean* by Ash Maurya
- *Lost and Founder* by Rand Fishkin
- *Hooked* by Nir Eyal
- *Psychology of Selling* by Brian Tracy
- *The Fire Starter Sessions* by Danielle LaPorte
- *Screw it Let's Do it* by Richard Branson
- *Will it Fly?* by Pat Flynn
- *The Start-up of You* by Reid Hoffman
- *Innovation and Entrepreneurship* by Peter Drucker

Most of these business and entrepreneurship books are available on Amazon and other popular online retail stores. The easiest way to see where to buy them online is to search their titles on Google.

Watch Entrepreneurship and Business Movies

Adapting an entrepreneur's lifestyle does not mean you should totally change your lifestyle. You only need to redirect your life to things that will help you achieve the goals you set. You shouldn't stop watching movies simply because you are living an entrepreneur's lifestyle. Movies are one of the ways to gain new ideas.

There are some movies that could help you as an entrepreneur. They change the way you reason, the way you see things, the way you react to new challenges, how to tackle new challenges. I personally recommend these movies for you:

- The Banker (2020)
- The Inventor: Out for Blood in Silicon Valley (2019)
- Becoming Warren Buffett (2017)
- Money Heist (2017)
- The Intern (2015)
- Steve Jobs (2015)
- Joy (2015)
- Walt Before Mickey (2015)
- Boiler Room (2000)
- Flash of Genius (2008)
- e-Dreams (2001)
- The Aviator (2004)
- Tucker: Man and His Dream (1988)
- Coco before Channel (2009)
- Beer Wars (2009)
- The Goods: Live Hard, Sell Hard (2009)
- Enron: The Smartest guys in the Room (2005)
- How to Get Ahead in Advertising (1989)
- Rocket Singh: Salesman of the Year (2009)

- Harishchandrachi Factory (2009)
- Manthan (1976)
- Guru (2007)
- Badmaash Company (2010)
- Baby Boom (1987)
- Margin Call (2011)
- The Pirates of Silicon Valley (1999)
- Freakonomics (2010)
- The Commitments (1991)
- Band Baaja Baaraat (2010)
- Jiro Dreams of Sushi (2011)
- Steve Jobs: One Last Thing (2011)
- The Startup Kids (2012)
- Chef (2014)
- Burt's Buzz (2013)
- Thank You for Smoking (2005)
- Two for the Money (2005)
- Something Ventured (2011)
- Guru (2007)
- Wall Street (1987)
- Night Crawler (2014)
- Pirates of Silicon Valley (1999)
- The Wolf of Wall Street (2013)
- MoneyBall (2011)
- The Pursuit of Happiness (2006)

- Office Space (1999)
- Catch me if you can (2002)
- The Shawshank Redemption (1994)
- The Social Network (2010)
- Forest Gump (1994)
- The Founder (2016)
- The Godfather (1972)
- Office Space (1999)
- Rocky (1976)
- StartUp.com (2001)
- Jerry McGuire (1996)
- Twelve Angry Men (1957)
- Wolf of Wall Street (2013)
- Rogue Trader (1999)
- Ctrl+Alt+Compete (2011)
- Lord of War (2005)
- Glengarry Glen Ross (1992)
- Risky Business (1983)
- The Call of the Entrepreneur (2007)
- The Corporation (2003)
- Boiler Room (2000)
- Jerry Maguire (1996)

Work Smart

If you want to work smart, you must always seek for better ways to improve a system. Don't base on your old ideas. Seek for new ideas. Be conscious of time, even If it means paying to have more time, do so. Spend more time gathering new ideas.

Always look for effective strategies to achieve a given task. When you win a new contract, don't rush to start work. Sit down and analyze the system, think up at least three different strategies to do the task. Then choose the most effective strategy. The most effective strategy must not be the one with the least cost, rather it must be the most efficient strategy that saves both time and cost.

Have a Positive Mindset

Most people fail because they had a failure mindset even before they actually failed. Do not have a doubt or double mindset. Tell yourself, "I must succeed this time". It will make you see success as not an option, but a goal which must be achieved.

Always Listen to your Mind

The mind is where most ideas come from. Listen to your mind, but don't fail to question it. Think over it before you act.

Entrepreneurs always have new ideas because they never stop listening to their mind, even if the last idea that came from it was never successful.

The Best Business Idea must not come from your Brain

When Mark Zuckerberg got the idea about Facebook at Harvard University, he called five of his close friends and shared his ideas with them. Three of them were not patient enough to hear him out. They left. Only two; Dustin Moskovitz and Duardo Saverin agreed to work with him and today, they are Billionaires.

Think over any new business idea you hear about. Don't reject it immediately. A friend will only reveal his business idea to you because he saw a potential in you and also trusted you. Don't be selfish while giving your own contributions. You might find an opportunity that will take you to the next level while giving a helping hand.

Have a Business Plan

Always have a business plan even before you start a business. This will help you evaluate your business to know if you are actually progressing. Feel free to update your business plan when the need arises. Revisit your business plan before you take any major decision.

The key elements of any business plan are:

- Executive Summary
- Company Description
- Organization and Management
- Market Analysis
- Products or Services
- Marketing and Sales Plan
- Operational Plan
- Funding Request
- Financial Projections
- Core Values
- Appendices

These elements may vary depending on the nature of your business venture. Also ensure your business plan is realistic. Don't just add features you know you could never cope with. Make sure it looks professional because investors will always ask for your business plan before finalizing whether to invest in your business. You could ask your business mentor to help you or seek the help of business plan experts.

Pay more attention to your marketing and sales plan because even if you produce the best quality product but don't know how to attract customers, your business is bound to fail.

Build a Brand Name

Have you ever wondered why different brands of the same product are sold at different price? That is the power of a brand name. While thinking of how to dive into your dream business, first work on your brand name. It will help you become more popular. You can retain your customers for a long time with a brand name.

There are different ways to build and grow a brand name. You could create a website, create a page on social media, But before you do so, you need to do these important things:

- **Choose a Name:** A good brand name should not exceed more than 3 words. Choose a phrase that is related to your business and it should be easy to remember.
- **Create a Slogan:** A good slogan summarizes your brand's purpose. It should be something unique that leave people with a positive feeling.

- **Design a Logo:** You also need a powerful symbol that will be associated with your products and services. It must not be a complicated design. Make sure people can easily identify your brand when they see the logo. A good tip is to include your brand name in the logo or its initials.

Don't forget to register your brand name as a trade mark as soon as you get started. You could register it with the United States Patent and Trademark Office (USPTO).

Build a Team of Like Minds

You will achieve more when you work as a team than as an individual who knows it all. Successful entrepreneurs are not those who know every aspect of their business, but those who know how to attract experts in various aspects of their business, bring out the best from these experts in order to achieve their goals.

If you want to own a construction company, you don't need to be the best architect, electrician, civil engineer. All you need is how to find experts in these various fields and work with them as a team. You need more of **leadership, communication** and **right decision-making** skills to succeed as an entrepreneur.

Act Now!

Don't wait for the best time. It will never come. Don't be afraid to make mistakes. Make mistakes and learn from them. They will make you stronger and more experienced. At first, mistakes appear to be set backs, but when you learn from them, they help you achieve something greater.

I have personally noticed that anytime I make mistakes and learn from them, I end up achieving something greater than I have planned beforehand. My first blog failed. But I learnt from my mistakes and started a second one which became very popular and successful. My first book was rejected. I learnt from my mistakes and wrote a second book, which was not very successful. I wrote the third book, it became more popular than the first two.

The first step is always the hardest. Don't wait for the perfect moment, create one. Just start, you learn a lot by so doing. Don't keep on reading inspiring and entrepreneurship books. Dive in and start swimming. You will gain more knowledge and experience doing so than just sitting down reading.

Start with the Resources you have

Most young entrepreneurs always give excuse that they don't have all the resources needed to start their dream business. There will never be a time you will have all the resources you needed. If the problem is getting enough capital, reduce the scale and start. But make sure you have understood how the business works before you start.

Avoid borrowing money to start up a big business you don't know much about. Rather start up the business with the available resources. Then when the business shows signs of success, you can now borrow money to grow and expand it.

Don't Give Up

Nothing good comes easily. Coca-Cola sold only 25 gallons in its first year. Don't give up because you did not achieve your business in the first year.

James Dyson went through 5,127 failed prototypes before he created the first successful model of the "Dyson Vacuum Cleaner."

Bill Gates' first company failed. He did not give up, instead he learned from it and started his next venture, Microsoft.

The truth is that 98% of entrepreneur never got a positive on their first attempt. So when you first business fails, learn from and don't quit.

There is a big difference between giving up and starting over. Winners don't quit, quitters don't win. A winner is just a loser who tried one more time. Look for better ways to do a task and always learn from your mistakes and failures.

If you feel like you are losing everything, remember that tree lose their leaves every year, yet they still stand tall, waiting for better days to come. Great things are not got easily. Time will test you to ensure you are fit for the level you are aspiring to attain. So be patient!

Challenges make you more responsible. Always remember this, "A life without struggle is life without success". So don't give and never quit.

There are some pictures that motivate and inspire me a lot. Among all of them, this picture of Jeff Bezos' office at Amazon in 1999 inspires me the most. I see myself going back to look at this picture anytime I lay my hands on my PC or felt like giving up because of some business challenges. Looking at Jeff Bezos sitting in that office, with all the books on that table, I see a very high enthusiasm and hope. I ask myself, **have you had such eagerness for this business? If Jeff Bezos gave up, will he be the richest man in the world today?**

Just take up to 5 minutes to study this picture. It will inspire you to keep pushing.

Jeff Bezos' Office at Amazon in 1999

NOTE: To **succeed** as an entrepreneur, you must first **improve**. To improve, you must first **practice**. To practice, you must first **learn**. To learn, you must first **fail**. To fail, you must first **try**.

You need to apply this tip starting from the end to the beginning.

In Summary, the 1% Entrepreneurs implement the **TRY strategy** to succeed in business:

- First, they **try** and fail.
- They **try** again and fail.
- They **try** once more and fail.
- They **try** a little different and still fail.
- They **try** again tomorrow and fail again.
- Then they **try** to find someone who has done it right (a mentor).
- They **try** to fix what is not working.
- Next, they **try** to expand what is working.
- They keep **trying** until they succeed.

QUESTION FOR YOU: How many times have you tried?

ENTREPRENEURSHIP SKILLS VS. JOB SKILLS

Is there any difference between the skills an entrepreneur possess and that of an employee? Sure, there is a huge difference. The gap is so much that it cannot be filled easily.

Entrepreneurships skills are not acquired within a short period of time, unlike job skills. You could take up a job after studying in the university. For jobs that require more technical skills, the company may give you a 6 month special training and you easily master the job.

It is not the same for entrepreneurship skills. It takes a lifetime to master all the skills you need to be successful as an entrepreneur. This is because as an entrepreneur, the more successful you are, the more knowledge you need to become more successful.

Best Ways to Improve your Skills as an Entrepreneur

One of my colleagues once asked me, "How did you gain your entrepreneurship knowledge"? Well, the answer I gave him was very vast. But I will summarize it here. The best way to gain more knowledge as an entrepreneur is through real life experience. You are only required to understand how a business works. But don't wait to understand everything before you dive in. Once you have carried out your research, ran your analysis and have got a good business plan, you are good to go. When you experience a new challenge, ask questions, carry out more research, be open-minded to other people's ideas. Being open-minded does not mean you should take every idea you get. Compare it with the ideas you had already.

Always listen to your customers, especially those who always speak out when they are not satisfied with your products and services. If you run an online store where customers rate your products and services, pay more attention to the bad reviews. They will help you improve.

The Best Time to Quit your Job

Many entrepreneurs take up a job in order to gain business experience and save raise funds to start their own business. It is a very good idea. Instead of taking loans from banks, you could pick up a side gig or part time job. It will help you stay away from debts while starting up your own business. But don't lose your focus. Set your plans even before you take up the job.

After graduating from Princeton University, Jeff Bezos worked with several firms before taking a very brave decision to move into the world of ecommerce. He quit his job in 1994. Not only Bezos, many other prominent entrepreneurs worked with several other established firm before starting their own firms. But how do you know the best time to quit your job?

Do not quit a job until:

- Your side income covers twice as much as your monthly expenses.
- Your emergency funds can cover your 1 year expenses.
- You are skilled enough to turn your side hustle into your main business.
- You are determined to work hard to succeed, about 12 to 16 hours a day without any excuse.

There are some signs that help you know when to quit your job. If you are no longer comfortable with your workplace policies, that is if the policies are affecting your own business plan, it is a sign. If you put more effort in your workplace and you are still not valued or if the job makes you live a rat-race life, it is also a sign.

HOW TO DISCOVER THE BUSINESS IDEAS THAT WILL WORK FOR YOU

Finding a business ideas is not a problem. The problem lies on finding a business idea that will work for you. That a particular business idea made some entrepreneurs rich does not mean it will work for you. There are many things involved in finding a feasible business idea.

Make Sure You are in the Right Business Zone

Stop looking too far. Develop a business that will depend on the skills you have already acquired and are an expert in. It will help you understand every aspect of the business model and put you in a better position to discover solutions to the challenges that may come up in the future.

You can explore your passion. Think of where you have worked in the past. What do you enjoy doing for the company? It could give you an insight. For instance, if you loved interacting with customers, then starting a coaching or consulting business may work for you.

Take Time to Study the Business Model

Every business has its own target customers, core capabilities, value configuration, etc. Are you able to meet the discrete requirements of the business you want venture into? Study every aspect of the business model. Do not neglect any aspect. Research on the business revenue models, value propositions and cost structures.

Check the Sustainability of the Business Idea

The two main factors that affect the sustainability of any business idea are demand and supply. A business idea will be sustainable if the demand is always higher than supply. Your product or service must not be a never-heard one in order to be sustainable. If the business idea already exists, offer something better than the existing solutions.

Also make sure that people will be willing to pay for your product. Just make sure there is something special that will make people choose your product in the midst of many alternatives.

Seek Advice from the Right Professionals

Make sure you take advice from business professionals, especially when it comes to business marketing because that is one of the key aspects of every business that will determine its viability and feasibility.

It is true that seeking advice from business professionals would save you a lot of troubles, but make sure you are asking the right expert that sees things from the same perspective with you. That a marketing professional told you that your business idea will not be feasible does not mean your idea was totally useless. He might be seeing your idea from the wrong perspective.

For instance, when Frederick Smith told his business professor about his business idea - FedEx, the professor gave him a C (average mark) and told him that his business idea would never work. But today, FedEx is one of the most admired brands in the world that survived macroeconomic challenges. The express shipping company has the world's largest all-cargo air fleet.

The problem was that Frederick Smith asked the wrong business professional. Don't rush to draw conclusion about the feasibility of your business ideas. Seek the advice of many business professionals. Some will encourage you while many will discourage you. Now, run your feasibility analysis with both categories of advice.

Can the Business Idea Solve a Problem in your Local Community?

You might be struggling to bring up a business idea that could change the world, whereas you don't see the people within you who need your ideas. That was how Mark Zuckerberg started. He tried to solve the social network challenge within Harvard University. On the long run, his idea also changed the world positively.

But how will you know if your business idea can change the immediate world around you? You can join groups where the recent challenges faced in your local community are discussed. This way, you will know if your idea could solve any of these challenges. Also, you can tell your friends and neighbours about your idea and ask them if it could solve any of their personal problems.

It must not be only your local community, you can check for ideas that could solve pressing challenges in your corporate job. Look at the challenges in the internal processes of the company; finance, marketing, sales, human resources, management, etc. Can your business idea bring a positive change in any of these sectors?

Your Lifestyle could Give You the Best Business Opportunity

Do you have much jewelries which your friends borrow for free? Do you know you could start making money by opening a business where you lend your properties to your friends and relatives for a few bucks? It must be jewelries. It might be shoes, fancy bags, clothes that you buy a lot. Many successful female fashion designers started this way.

There are many feasible business idea within you. Stop looking too far. Think about your lifestyle and those of your friends', your current and past workplace, your passion and your local community. Business ideas discovered within these settings are always lucrative and have a very high probability of success.

HOW TO USE SWOT ANALYSIS FOR EFFECTIVE BUSINESS PLANNING

I know you might have been hearing about SWOT analysis. SWOT as an acronym means Strengths, Weaknesses, Opportunities, and Threats. SWOT analysis is one of the strategic business planning tools that can help you as a business owner to identify your business strengths and weaknesses as well as the opportunities and threats to consider in order to make an effective business plan for a particular situation.

SWOT analysis is used often when making business decisions, especially those that pertain to marketing. The situations where SWOT analysis is applied is numerous. That is why you need to understand its concept and how to apply it to your own business, whether big or small.

Elements of SWOT Analysis

Generally, SWOT analysis is broken down into four elements:

- Strengths (S)

- Weaknesses (W)
- Opportunities (O)
- Threats (T)

You need to understand what each element actually means. So let's take them one after the other.

Note that before you carry out SWOT analysis, you must have an objective in mind. For example, SWOT analysis can help you know the implications of adding a new product to your business. Would it yield more profit or will it just increase the company's expenditure? These are some of the things SWOT analysis can help you know before you actually implement the plan.

To get the best realistic result from any SWOT analysis, you need to first do some research in order to understand your business, industry and market. A survey from your staff, business partners and clients could go a long way to help you in the research. You also need to know more about your competitors.

Strength

The first element of SWOT analysis. Think of anything your company is good at (internal positive factors). It could be:

- Your company's brand attributes.
- What your company does better than its competitors.
- Your company's unique skills.
- Advanced facilities your company has.

Just list these strengths as you remember them. Don't bother about prioritizing them for now. That will come later.

Weakness

The second element of SWOT analysis. This anything that puts your company at a disadvantage to others (internal negative factors). It could be:

- Declining market share.
- Unfavourable business location.
- Unclear unique selling proposition.
- Things your competitors do better than you.
- Resource limitation.

Opportunities

The third element of SWOT analysis. Think about possible external opportunities (external positive factors). Make sure these opportunities are not already listed as your company's strength. It could be:

- New technology.
- A change of government.
- Few competitors in your business location.
- Growing demand for one of the products your company produces.
- Press/media coverage of your company.

Threats

The fourth element of SWOT analysis. These are external factors that pose a threat to your business. It could be:

- Increasing competition.
- Increase cost or scarcity of raw materials.
- Uncertainty of global markets.
- Changing regulatory environment.
- Changing customer attitude towards your company's products.

How to Create a Prioritized SWOT List

You now have four separate lists, one for each SWOT element. It is now time to arrange the results in the list according to their importance to your business. The most important results should be at the top, while the less important should be at the bottom of each list and should be addressed last.

The best way to have an overall picture of the four lists at a time is to draw a rectangle and then divide it into 4 quadrants (known as grid-like matrix with four distinct quadrants), then place each list in a specific quadrant.

STRENGTHS	WEAKNESSES
• Your company's brand attributes. • What your company does better than its competitors. • Your company's unique skills. • Advanced facilities your company has.	• Declining market share. • Unfavourable business location. • Unclear unique selling proposition. • Things your competitors do better than you. • Resource limitation.
OPPORTUNITIES	**THREATS**
• New technology. • A change of government. • Few competitors in your business location. • Growing demand for one of the products your company produces. • Press/media coverage of your company.	• Increasing competition. • Increase cost or scarcity of raw materials. • Uncertainty of global markets. • Changing regulatory environment. • Changing customer attitude towards your company's products.

SWOT analysis quadrant

Repeat the above last step when you have arranged the results in the list according to their importance to your business.

How to Use the Results of SWOT Analysis for Effective Business Planning

Now that you have prioritized the 4 lists generated through SWOT analysis, it's now time to use these results to develop long-term and short term strategies for your business.

One of the best ways to turn these SWOT results into effective strategies is to consider how the results from the 4 lists overlap with each other. You will discover 4 effective strategies:

- **Strength-Opportunity Strategy:** Now study the results in both the strength and opportunities list and ask yourself; **which of my company's strength can be used to maximize the opportunities I have identified?**
- **Strength-Threat Strategy:** Also study both the strength and threat lists and ask yourself; **how can I use my company's strengths to minimize the identified threats?**

- **Weakness-Opportunity Strategies:** Now study the weakness and opportunity lists and ask yourself; **what actions can I take to minimize my company's weaknesses using the discovered opportunities?**
- **Weakness-Threats Strategy:** Finally, study the weakness and threats lists and also ask yourself; **how can I minimize my company's weaknesses to overcome the identified threats?**

Now include these strategies you developed in your company's strategic plan for your initial objective for carrying out the SWOT analysis. Don't forget to discuss the results of your strategies with your team, explaining to them the basis of your analysis and why it was a bit different from the initially planned strategy. These are some effective ways to discover more realistic strategies for business planning.

Why Every Business Needs SWOT Analysis

Most small business owners ask if SWOT analysis are practical or even feasible for their business size. Considering the numerous benefits of SWOT analysis in business planning and decision making, every business category and size needs to apply this analysis as often as possible, not only in major decision making, but also in minor decisions that might affect the business on the long run.

One of the benefits of conducting SWOT analysis is that it provides a golden opportunity for business owners to gain more insights on how their business operates and the extent to which their competitor's business strategies affect their own business.

HOW TO OVERCOME THE MAIN BUSINESS STARTUP CHALLENGES: CAPITAL AND RUNNING FUNDS

90% of new businesses fail because of lack of funds to run the business and improper fund management. Be it an online or offline business, financial management is the key tool that will determine if the business will succeed or fail. No matter how big your startup capital is, if it is not properly managed, the business will die within the first 5 years of its startup. An entrepreneur with a grounded knowledge of business financial management can take a small scale business to a higher level. Most entrepreneurs have nice business ideas but could not actualize it because of lack of funds.

Best Ways to Raise Fund for Business Startup

There are many ways you can raise capital for a new business. Let's explore some of them.

Find a Lucrative Part-Time Business

This is one of the best ways to raise funds for business startup. There are many online and offline jobs you could take up, just to save money to startup your own business. Also take the one that will give you time to plan your own business. You could also work full time with the business firm and then resign once you have saved enough money. Most entrepreneurs have switched back to employee lifestyle because of the offer they get while working with the company. Set your target right from the onset and be determined to achieve it. This was the strategy Jeff Bezos used before starting up amazon. You don't only save money while working for another firm, you also gain knowledge and experience.

Raise Money by Selling your Personal Asset

Do you have real estate properties or stocks? You could sell part of them to raise startup capital.

Take Advantage of Venture Capitalists

There are investors who are ready to invest up to 1 million dollar in fast growing businesses and technology firms. But you need to convince these investors that investing in your business is the best option. The best way to achieve this by having a good business plan.

Utilize CrowdFunding

If you have already started your business but need more funds to expand it, then crowdfunding is the best option for you. There are sites who offer financial assistance to young entrepreneurs who have met some business goals and need fund to grow. **CrowdFunder** is one of the popular platform.

Apply for Loans

Do you have a collateral that can cover for the loan amount? Then apply for one. Personally, I go for loans when I have no other option. Look for financial organizations that charge very little interest. If you don't have a collateral for a bank loan, you could also get a business loan through Peer-to-Peer platforms, where potential investors release funds to entrepreneurs with good business plan. Make sure you read and fully understand the pay back terms before taking the loan. I recommend *Prosper* and *Lending Club*.

Apply for a Business Grant

Grants are financial aids that are not meant to be paid back. They are often made available for young entrepreneurs who have good business plans. But the amount is usually small. You could augment it with your personal fund or funds you raised from any other source.

Beware of internet fraudsters that target young business owner. They claim to offer business grants, but will ask you to pay a fee to process the grant. Legit grants don't cost any money. Once your business meets the grant terms, you will get it.

Find a Business Incubator

There are organizations whose sole aim is to help young entrepreneurs both financially and morally. Make sure your business idea has a very high likelihood of success before joining these organizations. There is a list of U.S. business incubators at *nbia.org*.

Attract Investors

There are many ways to directly attract investors online. One of the easy ways is through blogging. Create a blog and grow it to become popular. Share business knowledge and ideas. When these investors come across your blog and read about your ideas, they will want to know more about you. So make sure you write more about yourself or your company and how you operate, your investment plans. Drop a contact, it could be an email address, Skype ID or office phone number. Email address and Skype ID are more preferable. Make your email address professional by using a custom email address that includes your blog domain. For example, "*admin@YourBlogName.com*". They will definitely contact you if your plans are reasonable.

Another way to attract investors is by attending big events and summits where popular investors and CEOs are invited. Make an impressive contribution. You could ask intelligent questions or smart suggestions. Always start by introducing yourself. You could meet some of these investors after the event to start building the network. Make sure you dress like a CEO because the way you dress is the way you are addressed.

You can search on Google about upcoming events and summit and how to reserve a sit. Some popular events and summits are:

- WebSummit
- TechCrunch Disrupt

- SXSW
- Collision

Tips for Saving Money at the Early Stage of your Business

Plan to start on a Small Scale

Do you have a business idea that need millions to startup? Scale it down. This is the strategy successful entrepreneurs use. When Bezos wanted start Amazon, he found 20 electronically marketable product, but scaled down from 20 to 5 and then to 1; books. Another advantage of starting a business on small scale is that you don't lose much if the business turns out unsuccessful.

Follow your Business Plan

Up to 50% of new businesses fail because they abandon their business plan. Your business plan should be your guide during the early startup years. Before you make any big decision, re-visit your business plan. It will help you know whether the new decision will help the business or not.

Do away with Unnecessary Expenses

When starting up a new business, you major concern should be how to minimize cost as much as possible. Make a scale of preference for all the company's needs. Then solve them according to their necessity and costs. You could even start up your business with fairly used machineries and equipment. But note that there are some equipment you should buy their brand new versions even at startup. For instance, your company's waiting room needs a new set of cushion. But you could start with a fairly used generator and then upgrade to a new one later.

These are some of the ways to ensure that the limited capital is utilized properly.

HOW TO BUILD A GOOD RELATIONSHIP WITH YOUR CUSTOMERS AND EMPLOYEES

The secrets behind any successful business is a good customer relationship and effective marketing. If you want to build a business empire, then you must learn how to attract customers, value and appreciate your customers. Entrepreneurs who apply good customer relationship strategies spend lesser money on marketing, but they still make huge profits. How is this possible? Their customers indirectly do the marketing for free.

If you want to attract new customers, first value your existing customers. It does not only end with attracting new customers, if you don't know how to retain your customers, then your business is bound to fall.

Why should you Value your Customers?

Here are some of the reasons:

Customers are the Kings

They are the reason why your business still exists. No customer, no business. That is why you should value them.

It is more Costly to Win New Customers than to Retain Existing Ones

Successful entrepreneurs know this and that is why they do everything possible to satisfy their existing customers. Once you lose one customer, your business profit will drop. Remember, there are tons of other companies offering the same products and service you do. Your competitors are on watch to win the heart of any customer you lose.

Customers' Adverts have the Highest Conversion Rate

Many times, I have bought a new product from a mall just because a friend recommended it. That's it. Your customers will only recommend your products and services if they gain enough satisfaction when they used it. But a customer who likes your product but hates your company's services will never recommend it to a friend. They will surely look for an alternative. Of course, the alternative is next door - your competitors.

Simple Rules for Retaining Customers

Do you wish to win your customer's loyalty? Simply apply these tips:

- Offer them discount
- Reward loyal customers
- Have an active customer support section

Best Ways to Appreciate your Employees

Apart from your customers, another set of people in your business you should value are your employees, those who work for you. They deserve more than appreciation from you. As you improve your Boss-to-Customer relationship, also improve your Boss-to-Employees relationship. The satisfaction your customers get from your company's products and services depends on your employees. They are also the people that make direct contact with your customers. You work with the feedback they get from your customers.

As you make budget for your business promotion, include your employees' appreciation cost in the budget. Workers can only put in their best when their employer values the effort they had already made. There are many ways to make your employee voluntarily go extra miles to ensure that your business grows.

One of my closest friends, Fred, a business owner has worked for a firm for more than 30 years and still works there. I asked him, "Why do you choose to still work with the firm". He answered, "I decided to continue working for the firm because of how they treat me. They treat me like a king".

You should generally appreciate all your workers. But there are some special set of workers that are more loyal than the rest. There are some criteria you should set so that you could easily pick out those workers that met them and reward them specially. Here are some of the loyal workers and how to spot them:

- **The Employee with the Best Customer-to-Worker Relationship:** Your customers are in the best position to help you pick them out. Ask your customers to vote.
- **The Most Punctual Worker:** You could go through your company's attendance register and pick the most punctual worker.

- **The Worker with the Highest Years of Service:** Your Company's workers' records will be helpful here.

Here are some of the simple ways to appreciate your workers:

Prepare a Get Together and Award Night

Most companies get together are scheduled at the end of the year or twice a year. Here's the best place to reward those hard working staff. Give them certificate of appreciation or recognition. This will not only encourage them to put in their best for your company's growth, but will also make other workers sit up.

Prepare a Work Shift for your Employees

If you have many workers, don't lay off some of them. Prepare a work shift roster for them. Rotate the shift so that some will work in the morning shift for a week and then join the afternoon shift the following week. You could ask your employee's opinion. Shift work schedule is most recommended for companies whose services are tedious. Employees who work on shift produce better output than those who work all day because they have enough time for themselves and then prepare ahead of time for the company's task. It ensures that the workers are fit, both physically and emotionally to face the task.

Offer Free Lunch

If your company is buoyant enough, offer free lunch to all the workers, but if you have limited resources, use it to appreciate those loyal workers. It must not be everyday, you could pick out 2 or 3 days of the week. You must not go for something very costly. A soft drink and snack could do. Just let your workers know that you appreciate their effort.

Social Media Recognition

Workers also want to be appreciated outside the company's wall. Use your company's social media page to announce the best worker of the week. Tell your social media fans to congratulate them. This appreciation strategy costs little or nothing, but your workers will value it so much.

Schedule Picnic or Game Time

It must not be all works throughout the year. Schedule time for fun. It could be biannually or quarterly. Take your workers out on picnic. Just raise up the idea, even if your company cannot carter for the whole costs. Your workers could help out.

You could also build game house where your workers could go for exercise. You could even generate income by collecting a little fee. Offer free ticket to those loyal workers. A gym center will be great!

These are some of the secrets some successful entrepreneurs have used to bring out the best from their workers, even without spending much. Your workers will put in their best when they are fit, physically, emotionally and mentally. These are some of the ways you could help boost their fitness. Then watch your company grow and your customer's being satisfied with your worker's services.

HOW TO CREATE SUCCESSFUL MULTIPLE PASSIVE INCOME STREAMS

If you want to be a successful entrepreneur, never depend on one income because entrepreneurship is full of risk and the best way to survive is to create multiple income streams. That is the only way you can be able to detect how your own economy will look like.

No business has 100% guarantee of continuity, you can increase its chances of survival, but not up to 100%. What if something unexpected happens to that one business and crashes the whole system, will you fall back to level zero? That is why successful entrepreneurs create multiple income streams.

Inasmuch as you should create multiple income streams, establish them one after the other. Make sure your first business is stable before you start the next. As you engage in more businesses, you gain more experience. The experience you gained from your business could help you easily overcome the challenges which may arise in the next one. If you try to startup multiple business at a time, you may end up achieving nothing. Once you successfully establish one business, you could easily establish another one.

Also, don't establish multiple businesses in the same business category. Diversify your businesses so that if crises arise in one business category, you will not back to your starting point. You could expand one of your businesses in a particular field. If it is an ecommerce store, you could add new products.

This was the strategy Jeff Bezos applied on Amazon that contributed to its popularity. After analyzing the annual web growth of ecommerce, Jeff Bezos created a list of 20 electronically marketable products and later narrowed the list to the five most promising products: compact discs, computer hardware, computer software, videos, and books. He decided to start with books because it has the highest demand and the least unit cost. He gradually added the other four products and the company continued expanding. Today, Amazon is the largest online store where you could buy anything you could think of. Had Bezos not narrowed his idea, Amazon would not had been successful and popular as it is today.

When Gary Vaynerchuk graduated from college, he worked 7 days a week for 5 years to grow his family's wine press to $60 million. He established other companies with the experience he gained from the wine press business and also published many best-selling books.

Various Forms of Wealth and Assets

In order to make the right decision as an entrepreneur, you need to understand the various forms of wealth.

- Financial wealth (money)
- Social wealth (status)
- Time wealth (freedom)
- Physical wealth (health)

Only entrepreneurship can give you all the four forms of wealth. Being an employee of having a job can never. Successful entrepreneurs avoid jobs because most jobs will lure you in with financial and social wealth, but rob you of time and physical wealth.

The four asset classes are:

- Owning a Business
- Real estate

- Paper, like stocks and bonds
- Commodities, like gold

Business Ideas for Entrepreneurs

There are tons of business ideas for entrepreneurs. I have taken time to categorize them into fewer numbers.

Buy an Existing Business

What could make a business owner offer his business for sale? Most times because it is not yielding the desired profit or may be it is running out of funds. A business might be unsuccessful because the owner does not have the right skills to manage and make the right decision.

Before deciding to buy an existing business, make sure you know why the owner offered it for sale. Make sure you can tackle the business challenges, else you will soon get tired of the business.

An existing business has a greater chance of survival because the brand name is already established. When you buy an established business, you inherit its brand name and even the market shares. You now concentrate on how to grow the business instead of being faced with the startup challenges.

Get a Franchise License

Little or more risk-proven system, it is expensive to get in most cases. When you buy a franchise, you are simply buying the right to operate an established business in another location through a licensing relationship, but you don't have full right over the business and its brand name. You, the *Franchisee* will pay royalties and must also abide by the franchise terms of agreement. You cannot implement a business plan that is against the policies of the *Franchisor*.

But you still save some startup costs. If the brand name is very popular, you instantly inherit recognition. Most franchisors will require you to pay a startup fee called *Franchise fee* before you can start operating under their trademarks and proprietary information. Some Franchisors give you an option to get the franchise from a third party financing agent, most times from banks.

Many entrepreneurs became successful through Franchising. But make sure you understand all the terms of agreement before signing. Also buy a franchise in a business line you understood how it works. The main advantage is that you could start up a business with lesser capital than you would need if you decide to start the business from scratch. But if you want to be your own Boss, then don't go into franchising.

Start a Business from Scratch

The best option, but it scares most young entrepreneurs. Of the four forms assets, establishing a business is the most challenging. Many entrepreneurs always say, "I don't have the resources or the required skills or I can't risk my family's life". For me, the pros of starting your own business from scratch outweighs its cons. But the truth remains that, 9 out of 10 new business fail within 5 years of startup. It takes time to build a business from scratch. At the early stage, it might require extra time; morning to night, but with time you will start working when you wish.

Most young entrepreneurs quit creating a business from scratch and fall back to the employee class simply because they don't have any means to pay off their daily bills. I encourage young entrepreneurs to always have a side business that will help them generate capital for the new business and also take care of their personal expenses.

A side business could be anything that takes lesser percentage of your time. You don't need to look far to find one. You could start one with the skills you have already or may need to acquire a special skill.

Here are some lucrative side businesses you should consider:

- Website Designing and Programming
- Life Coaching
- Online Virtual Assistance
- Machine Learning
- Blockchain Programming
- Pet Business
- Yoga Studio
- YouTube Video Blogging
- Freelance Graphics Designing
- Content Translating
- Freelance Ghostwriting
- Real Estate Investment
- Event Planning and Promotion
- Affiliate Marketing Partnership
- Drop Shipping
- Book Writing
- Blogging
- FAQs Chatbot Building

- SEO (Search Engine Optimization)
- Email marketing
- Domain Name flipping
- Forex trading (Foreign Exchange)
- Drone Videography
- Catering Services
- Travel Planning
- Fashion and Designing
- Agricultural Businesses: Plantation farming, Feed production, Farmers transportation, Poultry, Egg Hatching, Creating a market for farmers, etc.

You could turn any of these side business ideas into full time business. You could even employ others and pay them.

Be a Smart Investor

You must be smart to survive in the game. Whenever investing is mentioned, you remember only the stock market, where you buy stocks and hope for luck to be on your side. Investment is a full course, you need to have an in-depth knowledge in order to make a long term fortune from it. Some others pay those they call "experts" to manage their investments. If you really care about becoming rich through investing, then you need learn the rudiments of investing, when and where to invest. Investment is not a game of luck as many people think.

To survive in the field of investment, you need to read financial books that will upgrade your reasoning and decision making pattern. This was one of the strategies that Warren Buffett, one of the richest entrepreneurs in paper assets used to master the field.

Invest only where you understand how it works. Warren Buffett summarized the secret to his success as an investor. He said, "If I cannot understand it, I will not invest in it".

Some fund managers Tom Bailard, Larry Biehl and Ron Kaiser developed a behavioural model that assists investors understand their behaviours better. Based on the personal traits of investors, these managers classified investors into 5 major groups:

- **Individualists:** Those who are careful, confident and often take a do-it-yourself approach.
- **Adventurers:** They are volatile, entrepreneurial and strong-willed. They are

ever ready to take the risk and bear the consequences.
- **Guardians:** They are wealth preservers, highly risk-averse.
- **Celebrities:** Those that follow the latest investment fads.
- **Straight Arrows:** They share the characteristics of all of the above equally.

Of all the five groups, which one do you think will produce the best investment result? Of course, the Individualists.

In which group do you belong? Do not worry, even if you do not belong to the Individualists' group, you could still meet your investment goal if you learn how to manage your core assets in the proper way. Always look for ways to improve your investment strategies. Don't forget that you are in a competition with different experts and institutions who have more investment resources. But do not be discouraged.

Another way to learn secrets of investing is to be a long term investor. Time and personal experience will also inspire you to become a better version of yourself in the field.

Here are some Investing books that will help you a lot:

- *The Intelligent Investor* by Benjamin Graham
- *A Random Walk Down Wall Street* by Blurton Malkiel
- *Little Book of Common Sense Investing* by John C. Bogle
- *The Essays of Warren Buffett* by Warren Buffett
- *Rich Dad Poor Dad* by Robert T. Kiyosaki
- *Beating the Street* by Peter Lynch
- *The Only Investment Guide You will ever Need* by Andrew Tobias
- *The Little Book of Value Investing* by Christopher H. Browne
- *The New Market Wizard* by Jack D. Schwager
- *Your Money and Your Brain* by Jason Zweig
- *The Book on Rental Property Investing* by Brandon Turner
- *The Money Game* by George Goodman
- *Trading in the Zone* by Mark Douglas
- *Common Stocks and Uncommon Profits* by Philip Arthur Fisher
- *The Millionaire Next Door* by Thomas J. Stanley
- *Market Wizards* by Jack S. Schwager

- *Reminiscences of a Stock Operator* by Edwin Lefevre
- *The Richest Man in Babylon* by George Samuel Clason
- *The Most Important Things* by Howard S. Mark
- *Irrational Exuberance* by Robert J. Shiller
- *Common Sense on Mutual Funds* by John C. Bogle
- *How to Make Money in Stocks* by Williams J. O'Neil
- *Poor Charlie's Almanack* by Charlie Munger
- *You can be a Stock Market Genius* by Joel Greenblatt
- *Fooled by Randomness* by Nassim Nicholas Taleb
- *Liar's Poker* by Michael Lewis
- *Thinking, Fast and Slow* by Daniel Kahneman
- *The Four Pillars of Investing* by Williams J Bernstein
- *When Genius Failed* by Roger Lowenstein
- *The Warren Buffett Way* by Robert G. Hagstrom
- *Buffett* by Roger Lowenstein
- *The Little Book that Beats the Market* by Joel Greenblatt
- *Winning the Loser's Game* by Charles D. Ellis

- *The Alchemy of Finance* by George Soros
- *Beffetology* by Mary Buffett
- *Against the Gods* by Peter L. Bernstein
- *The Snowball* by Alice Schroeder
- *Principles* by Ray Dalio
- *The Big Short* by Michael Lewis
- *Unshakable* by Tony Robbins
- *What are the Customer's Yatch?* by Fred Schwed
- *The Clash of the Culture* by John C. Bogle
- *Money Master* by Tony Robbins
- *Extraordinary Popular Delusions and the Madness of Crowds* by Charles Mackay
- *The Simple Path to Wealth* by JL Collins
- *The Elements of Investing* by Charles D. Ellis
- *The Black Swan* by Nassim Nicholas

Most of these investing books are available on Amazon and other popular online retail stores. You could simply type their titles on Google.

Investing in real estate business is one of the best investment ideas with very little risk. Real estate business involves buying, selling or renting a property, building, home or land. The business could be further divided into:

- Loan servicing (you collect monthly payments, pay taxes and also take care of any other loan aspects until the loan is paid off, with interest)
- Residential properties (undeveloped land, houses, condominiums and town houses)
- Commercial properties (office buildings, warehouses and retail store buildings)
- Industrial properties (factories, mines, and farms)

All you need to get started is a good business plan, capital, registered brand name and experienced real estate agents.

To earn up to 100% returns from property real estate, buy the properties from developing areas where there is very low demand and high supply. Then market them in developed areas where there is very high demand and low supply. Entrepreneurs and investors in these areas are willing to buy these properties at any cost once you are able to convince them. Show them the development growth trend of the locations of these properties. You will also need a very effective marketing strategy. Make sure you have one in your business plan.

The 8 Income Streams for Entrepreneurs

One of the advantages of being an entrepreneur is that you have many chances of survival and can tap from multiple income streams. Income is generally divided into Passive and Residual income. Based on the various available income streams, here are the different income streams entrepreneurs can tap from:

- **Earned Income:** Income from a part-time job.
- **Profit Income:** Earned from buying and selling.
- **Interest Income:** Earned from lending money.
- **Capital Gains:** When your assets increase in value.
- **Dividend Income:** Income earned from buying and selling of stocks and shares.
- **Rental Income:** Income earned from renting properties.
- **Royalty Income:** Earned when others use your idea. The most common type is that earned from a book you wrote and published.

- **Residual Income:** This is the money is available after you have met all your financial obligations. Most times, it is affected by your total earnings and your financial obligations. If you must have a residual income, then your total earnings must be greater than the costs of your financial obligations.

INSPIRING BUSINESS QUOTES AND ADVICE FOR YOUNG ENTREPRENEURS

Here are some inspiring business wise quotes and advice for young entrepreneurs:

"The spirit of an entrepreneur is to be a risk taker, to be resourceful and unstoppable, and to have a vision of yourself beyond where you are and not willing to settle for life as it is" - **Les Brown** (Authority on Achievement and Author, Fight for your Dreams).

"Think about the great entrepreneurs as visionaries. They have heart. They are willing to do today what others won't, so that they could do tomorrow what others can't" - **Susan Sly** (Entrepreneur and Author, The Have it All Woman).

"Personally, I think about the new economy, the old economy and then create my own economy. The entrepreneurs are creators. I decide what the economy is going to be like" - **Bob Proctor** (Chairman, Proctor Gallagher Institute).

"In the world of entrepreneurship, there are no limit. You can make as much as you want, depending on how much you want to work and how smart you are, how great the team you put together" - **Kim Kiyosaki** (Entrepreneur and Author, Rich Woman).

"There is no war in lifetime and world in business than being an entrepreneur." - **Mark Victor Hansen** (Entrepreneur and Co -Author, Chicken Soup for the Soul Series).

"Anyone could be anything. But people want to give up their freedom and become effectively a modern day slave to what someone else tells them to do, 'leave your home by 5:50 am, report to work by 7:30 am' just to earn a living" - **Paul Zane Pilzer** (Economic Advisor for Two U.S. Presidents).

"There is something wrong. On Monday morning, the heart attack rate increases by 35%. Technology is accelerating. Job security is declining" - **Les Brown** (Authority on Achievement and Author, Fight for your Dreams).

"There is a better way of doing every aspect of our lives. But most times, we choose to do it the old way" - **Paul Zane Pilzer** (Economic Advisor for Two U.S. Presidents).

"On a global basis, everything is being turned upside-down because of the rapidly advancing technology. They are eliminating many jobs. Many people are not prepared the jobs that exist" - **Dr. O.C. Ferrell** (Professor of Marketing - University of New Mexico).

"The idea of job security and information is so obsolete. But the whole problem still lies on the school system. There is no financial education in school system. Students are solely trained to be employees. The income of the educated middle class is declining for years, yet people still go to school solely to get a job. Now what happens to the middle class people whose skills are off the track. They become what we call, 'the working poor'. The food stamp is increasing to the roof because most people cannot earn what we call, 'a living wage'" - **Robert T. Kiyosaki** (Entrepreneur, Educator and Author, Rich Dad Poor Dad).

"Most people have experienced financial pressures. They are probably greater these days, than they have been in the past" - **Jordan Adler** (Entrepreneur and Author, Beach Money).

"Today, if you want to control your future, the 40-40 plan is gone, where you graduate from college and work for 40 hours a week for 40 years. That day is gone" - **Les Brown** (Authority on Achievement and Author, Fight for your Dreams).

"The basis for life is worry; 'Am worried maybe I will get fired, am worried maybe my company will go out of business, am worried because I can no longer keep up with the growing bills, am worried about how I will send my kids to college, what if my car breaks down, am worried coz I can't fix it'. People live in a sea of worry and it eats at them" - **Richard Bliss Brooke** (Entrepreneur and Author, The Four Year Career).

"It's time to look in the mirror and say, 'it is not the economy, it is my economy, it is my little world where I am. I need to grow. Am not going wait for the economy to come back'" - **Paul Zane Pilzer** (Economic Advisor for Two U.S. Presidents).

"Everybody should be a business owner. I only tell people who are wounded spiritually to become an employee. It is a no way kindness when I tell somebody, 'you will be a great employee'" - **Chris Brogan** (New York Times Best Selling Author, Trust Agents).

"Behind every successful story, there is a river of tears, a mountain of obstacles, an ocean of impossible odds and unbreakable warrior spirit"- **Chatri Sityodtong**.

"Never think that you can start your business today and succeed the next year. My business took 10 years to feel that success" – **Jack Ma** (CEO, Alibaba).

"Rich people buy luxury last, while the poor and the middle class buy luxury first" - **Robert T. Kiyosaki** (Entrepreneur, Educator and Author, Rich Dad Poor Dad).

"Give me 6 hours to chop down a tree and I will use the first four hours sharpening the axe." - **Abraham Lincoln**.

Jeff Bezos once asked **Warren Buffett**, "Warren, your investment strategy is so simple; why is it that people don't emulate you?" Warren Buffett replied, "Because nobody wants to get rich slowly".

There are 3 types of people; those who work smart, those who work too hard and those who give up soon. You can work hard, but if you don't work smart, you will work till the end of your life.

Life is not about finding yourself. It is about creating yourself. Death is not the greatest loss in life. The greatest loss in life is what dies inside you while you are still alive.

A shark in a fish pond will grow only 8 inches. But in the ocean, the same shark will grow 8 feet or more. The shark will never outgrow its environment. The same applies to human minds.

Time is the only thing that will not cheat you. So use it wisely.

Business is all about solving problems for people. Your business will only succeed if your ideas can solve people's problem. They will be glad to pay you.

Your life is like a book. One bad chapter does not mean your story is over. There are better days ahead. Can you see them?

"You are never too old to set another goal or to have a new dream" - **Vivek Sharma**.

Age means nothing in business. Mark Zuckerberg founded Facebook at the age of 19. Bill Gates founded Microsoft at the age of 20. Steve Jobs founded Apple at the age of 21. Jeff Bezos founded Amazon at the age of 30. Ray Kroy founded McDonald's at the age of 56. Colonel Sanders founded KFC at the age of 65. How old are you?

Comfort is a drug. Once you get used to it, it becomes addiction. Give a weak man consistent sex, good food, cheap entertainment and he will throw his ambitions right out of the window. The comfort zone is where dreams die.

Do you wish to win? Focus on the game, not on the score board.

Stop complaining how bad the world is. Change the world. Find solutions to challenges like **Elon Musk**. Elon wanted a new payment method on the internet, so he created PayPal. He wanted an innovative electric car, so he invented Tesla Motors. Elon wanted to give people the chance to go to space, so he invented the Space X. Today he is one of the world renowned Billionaires.

Do you wish to raise future Billionaires in your generations? Teach them financial education. Give your kids $10 for every Personal development book the read. This will help them grow with a Billionaire's mindset. Don't give your kids $10 for every house chores they do, else, they will grow up with an Employee's mindset.

A QUIZ FOR YOU

If you are given these four options to choose one, which one will you choose? Tell me your reasons for choosing the option.

   a. $1,000,000 cash.
   b. Lifetime free travelling.
   c. Hangout with the richest person on earth for 2 years.
   d. 75% chance to win $500,000.

Tip: Your reasons are what will justify your answer.

Send your answer to me through this form: **http://eepurl.com/gdwj4P**

I will send you a personalized business advice based on the answer you chose.

CONCLUSION

Thanks once again for buying and reading my book *The Passionate Entrepreneur's Lifestyle*. Like I said earlier, not everybody will survive as an entrepreneur, but for a good startup, start with your passion. Even if you don't succeed with it, you will learn much lessons that will help you succeed in other business you may venture into in the future.

Do you want to succeed as an entrepreneur? *Do not be afraid of failure.* In fact, failure is an unavoidable aspect of entrepreneurship that scares many employees away from succeeding as entrepreneurs.

Even before you start any business, have a plan B. Your plan B will answer this question, **what step to take if the business eventually fails?** Never give this plan B a top priority, but make sure you have already concluded your escape route before you start the business.

If this book really inspired you or helped your new business, drop your testimonies on the amazon page of this book.

Follow my Quora space, **Lucrative Business Ideas** at **quora.com/q/lucrativebusinessideas**.

YOUR NEXT READ: ENTREPRENEURS MULTIPLE INCOME STREAMS GUIDES

Like I taught in this book, the only way to convert a dream to an achieved goal is by taking actions. I have made mention of many business ideas without much practical guides. In this book ***Entrepreneurs Multiple Income Streams Guides***, I will walk you through on how to earn a 6 figure monthly income from Investments, Book Publishing, Blogging, YouTube Videos, SEO, Fiverr, Dropshipping and other Digital Marketing.

According to Bill Gates, "Any business that does not base on the internet has no future".

The book is in the same series with ***The Passionate Entrepreneur's Strategies*** (*Lucrative Business Ideas Series*). It's available on Amazon.

Grab this book and put all the tips you have learnt in this book to practice. The book will teach you how to convert your passions into long-term income streams.

BONUS: FREE ENTREPRENEURSHIP RESOURCES FOR FURTHER INSIGHT

Below are the links to some free helpful articles on my blog. Check them out. Comment below any of the articles if you have any challenge. I will gladly attend to you.

Entrepreneurship Startup Guide & Business Advice

125 Inspiring Business Quotes & Advice from Successful Entrepreneurs -
https://www.buzzingpoint.com/2020/04/business-advice-for-entrepreneurs.html

7 Features that Distinguish Real Entrepreneurs from Job Seekers -
https://www.buzzingpoint.com/2019/12/features-of-real-entrepreneurs.html

5 Reasons Why You Should Value your Customers & How to Treat them -
https://www.buzzingpoint.com/2019/12/why-you-should-value-customers.html

5 Best Ways to Appreciate your Employees as an Entrepreneur -

https://www.buzzingpoint.com/2020/01/ways-to-appreciate-employees.html

Tips to Help you Write a Good Business Plan: Step by Step Guide -

https://www.buzzingpoint.com/2020/02/how-to-write-business-plan.html

12 Best Ways to Raise Funds & Save Money for Young Businesses -

https://www.buzzingpoint.com/2020/03/ways-save-money-young-business.html

30 Best Worldwide Small Business Grants and How to Secure Them -

https://www.buzzingpoint.com/2020/04/best-worldwide-small-business-grants.html

12 Tips to Help You Build an Efficient Email Marketing Contact List -

https://www.buzzingpoint.com/2020/04/build-email-marketing-contact-list.html

How to Start Peanut Burger Business: Production & Marketing Guide -

https://www.buzzingpoint.com/2020/03/peanut-burger-business-guide.html

How Life Insurance can Serve as a Lifetime Investment -
https://www.buzzingpoint.com/2020/04/life-insurance-investment-tips.html

Top 9 Ways Artificial Intelligence (AI) can Boost Business Productivity -
https://www.buzzingpoint.com/2020/05/how-ai-boosts-business-productivity.html

9 Best Sites to Buy Affordable SEO Optimized WordPress Themes -
https://www.buzzingpoint.com/2020/04/seo-friendly-wordpress-themes-sites.html

7 Best Cheap and Reliable Web Hosting Companies for Bloggers -
https://www.buzzingpoint.com/2020/04/best-blogging-web-hosts.html

7 Best WordPress Blog and eCommerce Themes to Download -
https://www.microsofttut.com/2020/04/wordpress-blog-ecommerce-themes.html

8 Working Steps To Writing Best Selling Books -
https://www.microsofttut.com/2017/11/steps-to-writing-best-selling-books.html

A Simplified Guide To Set Up, Self-Publish & Sell Your Books On Amazon -
https://www.microsofttut.com/2017/08/guide-to-set-up-self-publish-on-amazon.html

6 Legitimate Simple Ways to Make Money Online for Free -
https://www.microsofttut.com/2017/12/6-legitimate-simple-ways-to-make-money-online-free.html

9 Secrets To Getting An Approved Google Adsense & Why Your Applications Were Rejected -
https://www.microsofttut.com/2017/08/9-secrets-to-getting-approved-google-adsense.html

7 Simple Strategies To Increase Your Google Adsense Earnings -
https://www.microsofttut.com/2017/08/7-simple-strategies-to-increase-your-adsense-earning.html

Review Of Bluehost - One Of The Most Recommended Web Hosting Companies -
https://www.microsofttut.com/2018/05/bluehost-recommended-web-hosting-company.html

15 Simple Ways To Increase Your Website Traffic For Free -
https://www.microsofttut.com/2018/01/free-simple-ways-to-increase-your-website.html

How To Create A Professional Facebook Page To Promote Your Business -
https://www.microsofttut.com/2017/02/how-to-create-professional-facebook-page.html

How To Turn Your Facebook Page Into A Shopping Mall In 10 Minutes -
https://www.microsofttut.com/2017/02/how-to-turn-your-facebook-page-into-a-shopping-store.html

7 Things to Consider In Order to Build A Successful Blog/Website -
https://www.microsofttut.com/2017/12/things-to-consider-for-a-successful-blog.html

Skill Acquisition & Business Ideas

25 Best Lucrative Online and Offline Business Ideas for Students -
https://www.buzzingpoint.com/2019/11/lucrative-students-business-ideas.html

5 Best Lucrative Skills You Can Learn Online for Free -

https://www.buzzingpoint.com/2019/07/best-online-free-lucrative-skills.html

15 Best Websites You Can Learn Online Skills for Free -

https://www.buzzingpoint.com/2019/07/best-websites-learn-skills-free.html

12 Best Lucrative Agricultural Business Ideas: Beginners Guide -

https://www.buzzingpoint.com/2019/07/best-agricultural-business-ideas.html

20 Best Udemy Online Courses for Personal Development -

https://www.buzzingpoint.com/2019/06/best-udemy-online-courses.html

5 Best High in Demand Programming Languages to Learn -

https://www.buzzingpoint.com/2019/07/best-programming-languages.html

5 Best Websites to Learn Web Development and Programming -

https://www.buzzingpoint.com/2019/07/best-cheap-web-design-sites.html

7 Steps to Help you Start DropShipping Business Online Successfully -

https://www.buzzingpoint.com/2020/04/how-to-start-dropshipping-business.html

www.ingramcontent.com/pod-product-compliance
Lightning Source LLC
Chambersburg PA
CBHW070243220526
45465CB00004B/1502